Gift from Ray and

W9-CBS-547

PEARL HARBOR

NEVADA
ARIZONA
TENNESSEE
WEST VIRGINIA
MARYLAND
OKLAHOMA

FORD ISLAND

CALIFORNIA

PENNSYLVANIA

POSITION OF BATTLESHIPS
AT PEARL HARBOR
DECEMBER 7, 1941

Cornerstones of Freedom

The Story of
THE U.S.S. ARIZONA

By R. Conrad Stein

Illustrated by Tom Dunnington

 CHILDRENS PRESS, CHICAGO

Library of Congress Cataloging in Publication Data

Stein, R. Conrad
    The story of the U.S.S. Arizona

    (Cornerstones of freedom)
    SUMMARY: Recalls the events surrounding the
Japanese surprise attack on Pearl Harbor during which
the U.S.S. Arizona sank.
    1. Pearl Harbor, Attack on, 1941—Juvenile
literature. 2. Arizona (Battleship)—Juvenile
literature. [1. Pearl Harbor, Attack on, 1941-
2. Arizona (Battleship)] I. Dunnington, Tom.
II. Title.
D767.92.S83   940.54′26   76-26572
ISBN 0-516-04642-X

Most of the men on board the U.S.S. *Arizona* were asleep belowdecks. It was Sunday, and the huge battleship was docked at Pearl Harbor in the Hawaiian Islands. The few men on watch looked at the rising sun and felt the warm Pacific breezes. Tony Muncie, an eighteen-year-old crewman, told himself that it would be a beautiful day—the kind of day that brings tourists flocking to Hawaii. The young sailor had no idea that this day, December 7, 1941, would become a day that shocked the world.

Thousands of miles away at a Japanese naval base, Admiral Isorok Yamamoto nervously checked his watch. He calculated what the time was in Hawaii and nodded. More than two hundred Japanese airplanes were now winging their way toward Pearl Harbor. The planes had taken off from aircraft carriers. They were on their way to destroy the United States Pacific Fleet. Yamamoto, Japan's highest-ranking Admiral, had planned the entire operation.

Admiral Yamamoto was an intelligent man. As representative of the Japanese Navy, he had once lived in Washington, D.C. and had come to know many American generals and admirals. Yamamoto loved to gamble and had had a reputation in the American capital as an excellent poker player.

Now he paced the floor waiting for the first bombs to be dropped on a nation he admired. Yamamoto did not want this war. He knew America could build huge fleets of ships and planes and would soon overpower Japan. But the Japanese government was controlled by a group of war lords who argued that their islands were overcrowded and lacked natural resources. Japan needed steel, oil, rubber, and farmlands. The war lords insisted that Japan must expand and take over China, Indonesia, and the Philippines to gain the resources of those countries. But the Philippines were a colony of the United States, and China was her ally. The United States, with a powerful fleet based in Hawaii, prevented Japanese expansion. The war lords demanded that the fleet be destroyed.

Yamamoto pleaded for peace, but his pleas were ignored and he sadly planned the first battle of a war he believed his country would lose.

There would be no declaration of war. Instead Yamamoto ordered one swift surprise attack designed to destroy the United States fleet. Six of Japan's finest carriers were sent steaming toward Hawaii. The carriers were protected by two battleships and a dozen cruisers and destroyers. Yamamoto, the poker player, was playing with his highest cards.

～～～～～

Tony Muncie had been in the Navy for just six months. The *Arizona* was his first ship, and he was proud of her. He played guard on the ship's basketball team and looked forward to the coming game against the team from the battleship *Tennessee*. It was peacetime and there was little to think about except basketball games and the girls in Honolulu.

Even so, the winds of war blew hot over the Pacific that autumn. Tony noticed the deadly serious attitude of his shipmates while practicing gunnery with the *Arizona's* powerful fourteen-inch guns. The older sailors believed that war would come any day. But no one dreamed the Japanese would strike first at Hawaii. Their ships could not carry enough fuel to cruise to Hawaii and back, and no large striking force could sail those thousands of miles without being seen and reported by some ship or airplane. No, Tony thought, if war comes the Japanese will probably hit the Philippines first.

But Tony and his shipmates did not reckon with the strategy of the crafty Yamamoto. For months before the attack, his Japanese sailors had practiced refueling at sea. Then Yamamoto sent his ships along a course in the Northern Pacific where few ships sailed because of constant storms during the winter. Yamamoto's strategy had worked, and the Japanese fleet now lay unseen two hundred miles off Hawaii while airplanes loaded with bombs and torpedos sped toward Pearl Harbor.

Tony was on firewatch that morning. It was a routine, peacetime task. In case a fire broke out on deck, Tony was to sound the alarm and help the fire fighters. There was little danger of fire, so Tony walked to the bow of the ship. The *Arizona* was docked just a few feet from the beach off Ford Island—in the middle of Pearl Harbor. She was one of seven giant battleships tied up there, some two by two, others alone.

Tony could name each one of them without having to read the numbers on the sides of the ships. He saw the *Nevada*, the *Tennessee*, the *West Virginia*, the *Maryland*, the *Oklahoma*, and the *California*. Here was the heart of the United States Pacific fleet. The sailors called this line of ships "battleship row."

Tony placed his elbows on the rail of the ship and leaned over the side. The ships in battleship row were painted gleaming white. Their giant guns, looming out of turrets, looked like the horns of fierce beasts. But, somehow, the powerful ships looked peaceful in the morning sunlight, and Tony thought about writing a letter home.

Near Pearl Harbor a radar station manned by two Army privates showed some confusing blips. Minutes later the screen was covered with dots showing that hundreds of planes were flying toward Pearl Harbor. The excited privates called the duty officer.

"Relax," the officer said, "those are our own planes."

A flight of American B-17 bombers was expected to arrive from California early that Sunday. The officer assumed that the blips on the radar screen were American planes.

Tony Muncie heard the distant buzzing of airplanes, but he did not look up. He supposed it would be Army Air Force planes on maneuvers. Since war tensions were so great, training flights on Sunday were not unusual. Tony wondered if war would come. Perhaps not. Just yesterday President Roosevelt and Secretary of State Cordell Hull had spoken to two Japanese ambassadors in Washington. Perhaps the talks would settle the differences between the two countries and there would be no war.

The sound of airplane engines grew louder.

Suddenly an explosion thundered with so much power it seemed as if the earth shook. A black cloud of smoke billowed from Ford Island.

At first Tony thought it was just the Army practicing bombing, but why should they do this so close to the ships? Then he looked up. The air was filled with planes buzzing about battleship row like a swarm of angry bees. Tony saw flaming red suns painted on the sides of the planes.

"My God," he said, "it's the Japanese."

Others were not so quick to recognize the fact that they were under attack. Aboard the battleship *Nevada* a band and a Marine guard stood at attention ready to play the Star Spangled Banner and hoist the colors as they did every Sunday morning just before eight o'clock. Halfway through the playing of the National Anthem, the rear gunner of a passing Japanese plane sprayed the ship with machine-gun bullets. He hit no one, but his bullets ripped into the flag. The band stopped for a moment. Then years of discipline took hold and the men continued playing. The Marine guard stood at rigid attention, and no one broke ranks. At the conclusion of the Anthem the band leader or-

dered, "Dismissed," and everyone scrambled for cover.

A line of torpedo planes closed in on the battleship *Oklahoma*. No one was manning the anti-aircraft guns so the planes flew low and sped directly toward their target. Torpedoes dropped from the planes. They splashed into the water and darted toward the battleship where many of the crew members still slept in cots belowdecks.

Three torpedoes tore into the *Oklahoma*, and the explosions jarred all of battleship row.

Sirens on the other ships screamed. Excited voices shouted over loudspeakers: "We are under attack! This is no drill. Repeat. This is no drill."

Sailors poured onto the decks of the battleships. Some were still in their underwear as they rushed to the anti-aircraft guns. But ammunition for the guns was locked in steel compartments. With no one to shoot back at them, Japanese pilots flew so low that American

sailors could see their faces. One frustrated sailor threw a monkey wrench at a dive bomber.

The *Tennessee* and the *West Virginia* were tied up side by side along the shore of Ford Island. The *West Virginia* was on the outboard side and took five hits from torpedoes. The *Tennessee* was in between the *West Virginia* and the shore, so no torpedo could hit her; but two armor-piercing bombs from low-flying Japanese planes crashed through her decks and exploded inside the great ship.

Three minutes after the first bomb fell on Ford Island, a message was broadcast to the mainland that no one in the United States would ever forget:

AIR RAID, PEARL HARBOR—THIS IS NO DRILL.

On the deck of the *Arizona* Tony Muncie worked furiously passing ammunition to an anti-aircraft gun crew. Someone had broken the padlock of an ammunition compartment, and many crew members were now at their battle stations. Finally, Tony thought, we'll be able to fight back.

Before the anti-aircraft gun could start to fire, however, a line of Japanese bombers roared over the *Arizona* and released their bombs. Five bombs crashed through the deck of the ship. One of them exploded belowdecks in an area where the powder for the *Arizona*'s huge guns was stored. There was a thundering explosion. The *Arizona* erupted into an orange ball of flame. Men on neighboring ships saw the giant battleship jump halfway out of the water, then sink like a rock into the mud and shallow water off Ford Island. Only her upper decks, swept with flame, poked out of the water.

Other ships on battleship row took quick hits from bombs and torpedoes. Two bombs crashed into the *Maryland*. Torpedoes ripped open the bottom of the *California* and she began sinking in the shallow water. Smoke billowed from the *Nevada* after bomb hits. Cruisers and destroyers in the harbor were bombed and machine-gunned. Japanese planes even attacked the ancient battleship *Utah*, which was docked away from battleship row, and was used only for target practice.

Other Japanese planes hit airfields and Army bases near Pearl Harbor. At Hickam Field, Japanese planes found dozens of American aircraft parked side by side like cars in a parking lot. In minutes, Japanese machine-gun fire made flaming wrecks of the American planes. Also at Hickam, a bomb crashed through the roof of a mess hall and exploded inside—where hundreds of men were eating breakfast.

As the bombing continued, American forces recovered from the shock of the surprise attack and began fighting back. At the airfields men pushed undamaged fighter planes away from those that were blazing nearby. The undamaged planes, loaded with ammunition, were soon speeding into the sky to challenge the attackers. On battleship row anti-aircraft fire poured from the damaged ships. Machine-gun fire rattled even from the *Arizona,* which had broken in two and settled into the mud. Belowdecks, crews on the damaged ships worked desperately to keep their ships afloat. If a ship had been hit in the stern and water was causing her to sink toward the rear, the sailors flooded the forward compartments to straighten her out. On the decks, sailors fought fires, helped the wounded, and manned anti-aircraft guns.

As American sailors battled fires and Japanese airplanes, they suddenly saw a sight they could scarcely believe. The mighty battleship *Nevada,* though damaged by hits from bombs and torpedoes, was slowly pulling out to sea. As she sailed past the flaming wrecks of her sister ships the men on the decks cheered. Perhaps the powerful *Nevada* would be able to break out to sea, find the Japanese carriers, and blast them to the bottom.

But as the *Nevada* steamed toward the entrance to the harbor, a second wave of Japanese carrier planes sped toward her. Dive bombers fell from the sky and plunged down toward the moving *Nevada* like hawks seeking prey. In seconds, the brave ship was hit by three bombs, and the commander had to drive her into the beach before she sank and blocked the harbor.

The second wave of Japanese planes attacked the damaged ships of battleship row, but this time they were driven away by a barrage of well-aimed anti-aircraft fire. Only one Japanese plane managed to get through the barrage to put a bomb into the *Pennsylvania*, but she was in dry dock and could not sink.

It was two-thirty in the afternoon in New York. Many New Yorkers were listening to professional football games on their radios, as they did every Sunday afternoon. A team called the Brooklyn Dodgers was leading the New York Giants seven to nothing when the radio broadcast was interrupted to report that Pearl Harbor was under attack. Other radio reports telling of a disaster at Pearl Harbor filtered in. Some

Americans became furious and cursed the Japanese. Others wept, and many prayed. Even today, any American old enough to remember December 7, 1941, can recall exactly where he was and what he was doing when he first heard word of the surprise attack on Pearl Harbor.

When the last Japanese plane finally sped back to its carrier, the wreckage of the once powerful Pacific fleet was incredible. Almost all the ships still above water were in flames. The *Oklahoma* floated sideways in the water. The *California* was sunk, and the *Arizona* lay on the bottom of the harbor.

Tony Muncie swam toward Ford Island through water thick with oil. He reached the beach, took two steps, and fell to his hands and knees panting. The oil soaked his clothes and covered his skin, making him feel twice his weight. He had been lucky—just how lucky he did not yet know. The shock of the first bomb that had hit the *Arizona* had blown him overboard before his ship exploded into a flaming orange ball. Tony lived to fight again, but the ship he was so proud of and his many close friends on the crew remained on the bottom of Pearl Harbor.

At his naval base, thousands of miles from Hawaii, Admiral Yamamoto listened to radio reports from his fleet off Pearl Harbor. The attack had been an overwhelming success. Even he had not expected to crush the United States fleet so completely. Younger officers congratulated him for his victory, but Yamamoto could not share their excitement. He realized that he had won only the first battle in what would be a long war.

Two things troubled Yamamoto. First, there were no American aircraft carriers at Pearl Harbor so all United States carriers were safe. He believed that in this war, to be fought over vast areas of the Pacific, carriers would become far more important than battleships. But even more, he was afraid the American people would be so outraged over Japan's surprise attack that they would work together to defeat his country. He wondered what chance tiny Japan would have against a united and angry American people.

Yamamoto went to bed early, telling himself over and over again that this war had not been

his idea. He had a very difficult time getting to sleep that night.

In Pearl Harbor the American forces counted their losses. What had started as a peaceful Sunday morning had become a nightmare. More than twenty-four hundred American sailors, soldiers, and Marines were dead. Eighteen ships had been sunk, and more than three hundred airplanes had been destroyed or badly damaged.

After the last bomb had fallen, American sailors worked desperately to rescue other sailors who were trapped belowdecks on the sunken ships. Hundreds of men waited in watery, pitch-dark compartments while other sailors struggled to free them. The trapped men banged on walls to guide the rescuers. For days, sailors worked on the decks and under water, cutting through metal with torches until they could reach their trapped comrades.

But the men on the *Arizona* could not be helped. Her bottom lay in the mud, and her

decks roared with flame. The fire was so hot that no one could get close to her.

On Monday, December 8, President Franklin Delano Roosevelt asked Congress for a declaration of war. In one of the most famous speeches in history, he said: "Yesterday, December 7, 1941—a date that will live in infamy—the United States of America was suddenly and deliberately attacked by naval and air forces of the Empire of Japan..." The President's speech was interrupted many times by thundering applause. Even his political enemies in Congress now wildly cheered the President. All Americans united with Roosevelt and were determined to wage total war.

Pearl Harbor was the worst military defeat in United States history, but out of that defeat came spirit. "Remember Pearl Harbor," became a battle cry heard throughout the war. A popular song was written around the words. Exactly what Japanese Admiral Yamamoto had feared had happened. The American people, shocked by Pearl Harbor, would work together toward victory.

Congress granted the President a declaration of war, and three days later Germany, an ally of Japan, declared war on the United States. The world was plunged into the bloodiest war of all times. The war would end with the dawn of a nuclear age, when atomic bombs fell on the Japanese cities of Hiroshima and Nagasaki.

When the smoke cleared at Pearl Harbor, American engineers worked to salvage the damaged ships. One by one, the sunken and damaged ships were raised from the water, towed to dry dock, and repaired. Most of them would fight again. The *California,* sunk early during the attack on Pearl Harbor, would be with the United States fleet that recaptured the Philippines from the Japanese three years later. The brave *Nevada,* which had tried to break out to sea during the attack, would later shell the beaches at Normandy when the United States and her allies invaded Europe.

Five of the seven ships on battleship row were repaired and fought during World War II. The *Oklahoma,* beyond repair, was towed out of the harbor to be sold as scrap metal.

Tony Muncie's ship, the U.S.S. *Arizona*, remained on the harbor bottom.

On the morning of December 7, 1941, the *Arizona* had a crew of almost fifteen hundred men. Eleven hundred and seventy-seven of them died on that tragic day. Their ship became their grave, for the bodies of the men were never removed. The Navy built a platform with a flagpole over the wreck of the *Arizona*. Every day during World War II sailors rowed to the platform and raised and lowered the flag in honor of her crew.

The U.S.S. *Arizona* Memorial, built over the spot where the *Arizona* lies, was dedicated in 1962. Thousands of tourists visit the shrine

every month. Some of them are men who were
stationed at Pearl Harbor at the time of the attack. Others served in other battles of World
War II. Many visitors are children and grand-
children of World War II veterans.

Those who come to pay their respects to the
crew of the *Arizona* think of the many men
below the shrine who died so suddenly and
while they were so young. Many visitors offer a
silent prayer.

The U.S.S. *Arizona* was stricken from the
Naval Vessel Register a year after the attack.
But the names of her fallen crew appear inside
the memorial. Those who died on that tragic day
of December 7, 1941, will never be forgotten.

About the Author:

R. Conrad Stein was born in Chicago. In the late 1950s he graduated from high school and served for three years in the Marine Corps. After his discharge, he attended the University of Illinois and received a degree in history. Mr. Stein now lives in the town of San Miguel de Allende in Mexico, where he teaches creative writing and juvenile literature at a small English-language college called the Instituto Allende. He is the author of many other books for young people published by Childrens Press and other publishers.

The author wants the reader to know that the character of Tony Muncie is fictional. The author felt that the events at Pearl Harbor could be portrayed with greater action when seen through the eyes of this fictional character. All the other events of the story are true.

About the Artist:

Tom Dunnington divides his time between book illustration and wildlife painting. He has done many books for Childrens Press, as well as working on textbooks, and is a regular contributor to "Highlights for Children." He is at present working on his "Endangered Wildlife" series, which is being reproduced as limited edition prints. Tom lives in Elmhurst.